WHISKEY MADE ME DO IT

60 WONDERFUL WHISKEY AND BOURBON COCKTAILS

LANCE J. MAYHEW
ILLUSTRATED BY RUBY TAYLOR

Andrews McMeel
PUBLISHING®

Andrews McMeel Publishing
a division of Andrews McMeel Universal
1130 Walnut Street, Kansas City, Missouri 64106

www.andrewsmcmeel.com

19 20 21 22 23 HPL 10 9 8 7 6 5 4 3 2 1

ISBN: 978-1-5248-7177-2

Library of Congress Control Number: 2021939283

ATTENTION: SCHOOLS AND BUSINESSES

Andrews McMeel books are available at quantity discounts with bulk purchase for educational, business, or sales promotional use. For information, please email the Andrews McMeel Publishing Special Sales Department: specialsales@amuniversal.com.

DISCLAIMER:

This book features recipes that include the optional use of raw eggs. Consuming raw eggs may increase the risk of food-borne illness. Individuals who are immunocompromised, pregnant, or elderly should use caution. Ensure eggs are fresh and meet local food-standard requirements.

Please drink responsibly.

CONTENTS

INTRODUCTION

"I like whiskey and bourbon and Scotch."

I can't tell you how often I hear that statement, but in reality, bourbon and Scotch are both types of whiskey. Just as the word "beer" is a broad-based word—including ales and lagers—whiskey is a catch-all for spirits made from cereal grains that have (usually) been matured in a wooden container.

The world of whiskey can be a little confusing, but this book should help you understand its many forms and production methods. A good place to start is to imagine whiskey as beer that has made a leap for immortality. Grain, water, and yeast are the backbones of both beer and whiskey, the difference being that beer uses hops, while whiskey is distilled to concentrate the flavors and alcohol.

Whiskey has a long history, particularly in Scotland and Ireland, its veritable homes. So, which country invented whiskey? It's an argument that you'll hear in bars around the world, but the best advice is to credit the Irish when in Ireland and the Scots when in Scotland. While distillation is much older than whiskey, distilling technology reached both Scotland and Ireland around the 15th century. The first distilling would have been done by monks, who, having tasted distilled spirits, or *aquae vitae* (Latin for "water of life"), in Europe, would have filled their stills with beer brewed at the monasteries to produce the first iterations of whiskey. These efforts were called *uisce beatha* (pronounced "OO-SKAY BAY-Tha") in Gaelic, meaning water of life. The whiskies produced then would have been unrecognizable to modern consumers; they would have been harsh and unaged, for drinking in the near future rather than allowed to quietly age. *Uisce beatha* slowly became *usquebaugh* in the 1600s, before being shortened to *usque*, which has a pronunciation similar to our modern "whiskey."

A quick aside on "whiskey" or "whisky"—the correct spelling depends (usually) on the country in which it is made. The Scots spell it whisky, and the Canadians and Japanese follow that custom. The Irish use the "ey" spelling, as does the United States, but exceptions exist, such as the Tennessee whiskey, George Dickel Whisky—spelled the Scottish way, as Mr. Dickel was convinced his whisky was as good as anything produced in Scotland. You'll find both spellings in this book, to respect the naming traditions of each whisk(e)y-producing country.

Tasting and nosing spirits is a challenge for most people. Of course, there are times when one can simply enjoy a whiskey without doing an *organoleptic analysis* of the spirit (yes, nosing and tasting has a proper name—you can win bar bets with this knowledge).

Pour yourself a small dram of whiskey (there is specialized glassware such as the Glencairn glass that is great for making the aromas and flavors more apparent, or just use a wine glass or Cognac snifter). Note its color, which can be a clue as to what kind of barrel it was matured in—a red tint can indicate a Scotch whisky matured in a sherry butt, while a more golden color is often indicative of an ex-bourbon barrel. Slowly tilt the glass and run the liquid along the inside, watching how it moves. If the spirit appears to cling and looks a bit viscous, the remnants that slowly move back down (called the "legs") indicate an older whiskey, whereas young whiskies will run right back down the glass. Keeping your nose above the glass (about an inch above the rim), inhale through your nostrils and breathe out through your open mouth. This is where the first aromas and clues about the whiskey present themselves—the influence of the cereal grains, the type of wood, and the environment in which it was matured. If you detect aromas of burnt plastic or cat piss (a real defect in poorly distilled whiskey), brace your palate for the assault to come. Feel free to download a whiskey aroma wheel from the internet to help you identify flavor notes.

Next is the first sip. This isn't a real sip, this is a small amount taken into the mouth so as not to shock the palate with a big hit of alcohol. Slowly move this around, through your teeth and gums and over your tongue, to get your palate ready for the second sip. Think about the flavors this sip presents when it hits your tongue. Often the entry, as we call it, is more fruit forward, followed by cereal grains, before wood notes start to show up. Each whiskey is unique, so let it reveal itself to you on its terms, not yours. The best part of tasting whiskey comes at the finish. In order to experience this, you must swallow the whiskey. After swallowing, breathe out and note the various flavors and how long these sit on your palate. Some whiskies have very quick and light finishes, whereas others can linger pleasantly on the tongue, revealing more layers and complexity even after they are long gone.

WHISKEY BASICS

Cereal grains are used to make whiskey. These make up the primary source of flavor before maturation. Some whiskies, like single malt Scotch whisky, are made from 100% of a single grain—in this case, barley—while others, like bourbon, use a mash bill (a blend of grains). A bourbon mash bill has to be 51% corn by law, with other grains, notably rye, wheat, and malted barley (barley that has been allowed to just germinate before being stopped immediately to take advantage of the extra sugars present). Even some less-common grains, such as millet or rice, can be distilled into whiskey. The bottom line is all whiskey is made from cereal grains, and how they are used (malted versus unmalted, and a single variety versus a blend of multiple grains) affects the flavors in the finished product.

Yeast is a very important part of every whiskey and a number of major distillers have a proprietary yeast that they use exclusively. (They often keep freeze-dried samples offsite in multiple locations in case a disaster affects the distillery.) Other producers purchase freeze-dried yeasts and some distillers are experimenting with a variety of unusual yeasts such as Belgian ale yeast. Yeast is used in one of the first steps of whiskey production, as the grain and warm water and yeast are combined to begin fermenting, when the yeast turns the sugars in the cereal grains into alcohol.

Water is also a very important part of whiskey production and almost every great distillery is located on or near a pristine water source—a spring, a lake, or a river. The great bourbon whiskey producers are renowned for the quality of the limestone water that trickles up through springs in Kentucky. In Japan, the Ministry of Environment has designated the water sources for Suntory Whisky's brand as being among the "most precious" in the country. The distilleries in Scotland, Ireland, and Canada are no different. The unique pH for each water source brings out certain flavor profiles in each whiskey.

Maturation occurs primarily through oak barrels, but the size of the barrel, whether it is new oak or has been used before, what kind of oak and how long it is used for aging, all affect the final flavors of a whiskey. Some distillers use more unusual techniques for maturation, from sending their barrels to sea on ships, to playing music to it as it rests, but it's the magic that happens in the barrel that allows the whiskey to mature. Many attempts have been made to speed up the maturation process, including using high pressure, ultrasound, or other techniques to fake the effects of barrel aging. None have successfully replicated the correct flavor profile.

Climate plays a major role in whiskey maturation. In hot Kentucky, where new oak barrels are stored in tin-sided "rickhouses," the heat creates an angel's share (evaporation of liquid in the barrel) that can reach 10% in year one, as the liquid seeps into the porous wood staves, and can average 4% per year for the remainder of its maturation. In contrast, Scotland, which experiences a much lower average summer temperature, allows distillers to write off 2% per year to the angel's share.

Other factors are affected by the climate; in an environment with warm temperatures and high humidity, more alcohol will evaporate out of the barrel than water, lowering the ABV as it matures, while in a lower-humidity environment water evaporates, which raises the ABV.

The kind of still used and how many times a product is distilled affect the final whiskies. There are essentially two types of stills:

The **pot still** is the older, less-efficient method of distillation. Modern pot stills are steam heated or occasionally heated by fire. The shape of the still is a good indicator of the type of whiskey it is producing— a short, round still with a short neck will produce a fatter, more full-flavored whiskey, while a taller, thinner still with a long neck produces a milder, gentler whiskey. A pot still works in batches, and one distillation can achieve an ABV maximum of 40–80%. Pot-still whiskies are generally distilled twice, and sometimes three times. A mixture called "distiller's beer" or "wash" is put into the still, which is a cloudy liquid that remains after fermentation. The first distillation yields what are known as **low wines**, usually around 20% ABV. The resulting liquid is then put into a second pot still (or the first still is reused), and second distillation with heads and tails cut (known as feints and fore shots) has to be made to ensure that only the heart of the run is captured. Any liquid left behind in the still (sometimes called pot ale) is discarded or turned into animal feed.

The **column still**, also known as the continuous still or Coffey still, consists of two columns that continuously distill the spirit. The first column has the wash pumped in from the top while steam comes up from below. A series of either bubble plate or a packing material inside helps the fractional distillation. The second still, the rectifier, condenses the alcohol vapors into liquid form. A column still is much more efficient, being able to distill to a 96% ABV, or as close as can be achieved without the use of chemicals or specialized lab equipment. While this still can be run constantly and extract a purer base alcohol, it does mean less flavor comes through.

STYLES OF WHISKEY

As France is to wine, Scotland is to whiskey—or whisky, as it is spelled outside of the US and Ireland! No true connoisseur can ignore the variety and depth of the whiskies produced there. **Scotch whisky** comes in five different styles, but around 90% of all that is produced in Scotland is blended. To be labeled as Scotch whisky, it must be distilled in Scotland from water and malted barley and may include other cereal grains. It can be distilled to no more than 94.8% ABV. The whisky must be matured for a minimum of three years in oak casks not larger than 700 liters, then bottled at a minimum alcoholic strength of 40% ABV. Scotch whisky allows the addition of caramel coloring for color correcting.

This is a good moment for a note on **barrels**. The majority of casks used for maturation of Scotch whisky (about 97% of Scotch maturing at any time) are ex-bourbon barrels made from American oak (*Quercus alba*). By American law, bourbon barrels can only be used once, so the majority are broken down and the staves shipped to Scotland. The staves are then rebuilt into barrels, with new ends added, and re-charred to release more wood sugars. This can be done many times during the useful life of a barrel (thirty-plus years), but the first time it is used to hold Scotch whisky is referred to as a first-fill barrel (the most esteemed by whisky enthusiasts). This has the greatest bourbon influence, which depletes as the barrel is reused. Sherry butts represent the majority of the other casks used to mature Scotch whisky and are much larger, at 600 liters. Other barrels are often used to "finish" a whisky for thirty to ninety days at the end of its maturation, when the whisky is transferred to a new barrel for a short time to pick up some of its characteristics. This will be labeled "rum cask-finished" or "Gaja Barolo barrel–finished."

Peat is one of the most divisive flavor compounds in Scotch whisky. Many people adore it for the smoke and phenol compounds with which it can imbue malted barley, but some find it an acquired taste. I come down firmly in the "adore" category.

So why is peat in whisky? Simply put, peat is an accumulation of decayed vegetation that forms in bogs. In older times, malted barley would have dried on screens set over burning peat, for the smoke to add its distinctive flavor. Peat is also close to the concept of terroir (flavors that reflect the unique environment of each wine), because various areas have different types of peat based on what grew there thousands of years ago.

BLENDED SCOTCH WHISKY makes up the large majority of Scotch whisky sold worldwide. This style was created when whisky merchants and grocers in the 19th century realized that by mixing single malts, which were rougher and more inconsistent, with relatively new grain whiskies (made from corn or wheat) produced on column stills, they could create a consistent house style that was generally lighter and sweeter and more marketable to a broader range of consumers. Today, master blenders still strive to recreate the same flavor profile of a particular whisky year in and year out. If an age statement is listed on the label of a blended Scotch whisky, it must reflect the age of the youngest whisky in it. The average ratio of grain whisky to single malts runs from 60–85% grain whisky to 15–40% single malts.

SINGLE MALT SCOTCH WHISKY is the second-largest category of Scotch sold worldwide. A single malt must be made from malted barley and distilled in a pot still, usually twice. It has to be made at a single distillery, where it is blended to create a harmonious whole to reflect that distillery's style. There are five official regions for single malt whisky in Scotland, although a sixth, the "Islands," is unofficially argued by many whisky enthusiasts:

The Lowlands—The whiskies produced in the southernmost area of Scotland are gentle and sweet. Some have been affectionately referred to as "breakfast whisky" because of the regional tradition of triple distilling, which results in a lighter style.

The Highlands—Physically the largest whisky-producing region in Scotland, its size allows for a variety of styles, from peaty and large to light and floral.

Speyside—This area features the most densely concentrated number of distilleries within its small borders. With production centered on eight locations—Strathisla, Livet, Findhorn, Rothes, Dufftown, Deveron, Lossie, and Speyside Central—the whiskies are generally light and fruity with some grassy characteristics, with a greater influence of sherry casks than in other regions.

Campbeltown—This is the only town to be its own whisky region. At its peak, the area featured thirty-plus distilleries, all producing powerful whiskies known for their smoke and salinity balanced by fruit and chocolate notes. Now only three remain.

Islay (pronounced *EYE-luh*)—The southernmost island in the Inner Hebrides is home to eight distilleries that produce some of Scotland's most iconic whiskies. As a general rule, these are big, peaty, smoky drams, with sea spray and an underlying sweetness. Geographically, the distilleries on the northern part of the island produce less peaty malts without the salinity of their southern counterparts.

The Islands—Included within the Highlands and not yet recognized as a separate region, the Islands deserve their own category, as their whiskies are unique—ranging from big, briny, and peaty to soft and floral, all with their own characters influenced by their location.

BLENDED MALT SCOTCH WHISKY is a newer style, which was known as vatted malt prior to 2009. Essentially a blend of only single malts (no grain whisky), these aren't common but many are excellent.

SINGLE GRAIN SCOTCH WHISKY is made from either corn or wheat and barley (it must include barley) in a column still in Scotland. These don't appear on the market very often but many are quite good.

The single grain designation refers to one distiller producing it—grain indicates a mix beyond barley has been used.

BLENDED GRAIN SCOTCH WHISKY is similar to single grain Scotch whisky, except that it contains whiskies from at least two different distilleries blended together.

IRISH WHISKEY is experiencing a renaissance not seen since the early 20th century, with eighteen distilleries now operating in Ireland and at least a dozen more in the planning. Irish whiskey is the only country-specific whiskey that is actually made in two countries within one island—the Republic of Ireland and Northern Ireland (part of the United Kingdom). Irish whiskey is made from malted barley (other cereal grains can be added) and must be distilled to no more than 94.8% ABV, aged in oak casks not larger than 700 liters for a minimum of three years, matured in Ireland, and bottled at not less than 40% ABV. It is usually triple-distilled, which results in a light, fruity, and sweet style. The use of peat in Ireland is rare, although these whiskies do exist. Like Scotch whisky, the age stated on the label must indicate the youngest age of the whiskes included. The majority of barrels used for maturation are ex-bourbon barrels, with sherry butts and wine casks sometimes used. Irish whiskey allows for the use of caramel coloring for color correction.

There are four types of Irish whiskey:

Irish Malt Whiskey—This is made using 100% malted barley and triple-distilled in pot stills. An Irish malt whiskey from one distillery can be labeled as an Irish single malt.

Irish Pot Still Whiskey—This is a blend of malted and unmalted (also known as green) barley. A minimum of 30% of each type of barley must be used and up to 5% of other cereal grains. Traditionally triple-distilled, this used to be the most popular style of whiskey in the world during the 19th century. If distilled at one distiller, the term single Irish pot still whiskey can be used.

Irish Grain Whiskey—This is made with no more than 30% malted barley, along with other unmalted cereals such as barley, corn, or wheat, and distilled in column stills. Those produced at one distillery can be labeled single grain whiskey.

Irish Blended Whiskey—These make up the vast majority of Irish whiskies sold. Confusingly, any combination of two or more styles of malt, pot still, and grain whiskies qualifies as an Irish blended whiskey, but the majority feature a dominant combination of grain and pot still whiskies.

JAPANESE WHISKY traces its roots back to 1870 but really began in its modern form in the 1920s. It is said to model itself on Scotch whisky, although some rice whiskies are produced too. In Japan, if a distillery wants to produce a blend, they make many different styles in-house or under the umbrella of a company, usually grain whiskies from column stills and pot still–based single malts, then blend these disparate whiskies into a house style. Japanese single malt whiskies are 100% malted barley (often imported from Scotland) and double-distilled in pot stills. Occasionally, Japanese oak barrels (called mizunara oak) are used, but they are very expensive and tend to leak; however, they do add a complex cedar spice component.

CANADIAN WHISKY can be made from any cereal grain or grain products (wheat, rye, and corn being the most common) and are aged in "small wood" of not more than 700-liter casks for a minimum of three years. The product must be distilled and matured in Canada and not bottled at less than 40% ABV. Many styles of Canadian whisky allow caramel coloring for color correcting, but they also allow up to 9.09% of flavoring to be added as long as it is a spirit aged at least twenty-four months or a wine. Generally, Canadian whiskies are a blend of base whiskies produced in column stills to a high proof then matured in used barrels, blended with flavoring whiskies.

These are generally distilled to a lower ABV on column stills, then possibly in a pot still, before being matured in ex-bourbon, ex-rye, or virgin-wood barrels. Both styles are generally distilled and matured from one grain at a time, then blended to create a house style. Barrels may be new or used, charred or uncharred. Canadian whisky is often referred to as "rye" because it traditionally contains rye in the blend (dating back to German and Dutch immigrants adding rye to the wheat mash), but wheat is most widely used. Now Canada is home to eight major distilleries and a number of small micro-distilleries.

AMERICAN WHISKIES include several styles that are distinctive to the United States, including bourbon and Tennessee whiskey, although it was rye whiskey that was first distilled by German and Scottish immigrants in Maryland and Pennsylvania. Settlers then moved into Kentucky and Tennessee, where corn grows well and water filters up through a natural limestone shelf, and where the majority of American whiskey production still occurs.

The "rules" for American whiskies (a catch-all name for all whiskies distilled in the United States) are that they must be distilled to no more than 95% ABV from cereal grains and stored in oak barrels. Mash bill is the most common recipe for American whiskies, which must then be bottled at no less than 40% ABV. To be labeled as a straight whiskey, it must be aged for a minimum of two years and have no additives.

These are very broad regulations, so let's take a look at American whiskey categories.

American Blended Whiskey—This is very popular, due in part to its use in cocktails like the 7&7 (Seagram's 7 Blended American Whiskey and 7 Up). It has to contain at least 20% straight whiskey, with the rest as neutral spirits (think vodka) or whiskey that doesn't qualify as straight whiskey, or a mix of both.

American Spirit Whiskey—This type is so-named as a ghost of most whiskies, containing only 5% of the real stuff with the remaining 95% being neutral spirits. Rarely seen.

American Light Whiskey—An outlier among whiskey regulations, this specifies that it must be distilled over 80% ABV and can be stored in either used or uncharred oak barrels. Rarely seen.

American Bourbon Whiskey—This was declared the United States' native spirit by an Act of Congress in 1964. While widely assumed to be made only in Kentucky (the majority is produced there), it can be made anywhere in the country. Bourbon has to be made with a minimum of 51% corn, although mash bills usually include 70–80% corn with the remainder a combination of malted barley and rye or wheat. Four-grain mash bills containing both wheat and rye along with corn and malted barley are rare. Wheated bourbons are sweeter and gentler whiskies, while rye-heavy bourbons are spicier with a cinnamon note. Bourbon must be distilled to no more than 80% ABV using either a column or pot still, or a combination of both. Many bourbon stills start with column distillation and then go into a "doubler" or "thumper," a variation of a pot still. Once bourbon comes off the still, the new-make spirit, called "white dog," must go into a new charred American oak barrel. Barrels cannot be reused for bourbon, but there is a loophole as no period of time is specified—any contact with wood, even for as little as fifteen seconds, transforms white dog into bourbon. Most bourbons are aged from two to six years—some longer—and to be labeled as straight bourbon whiskey, it must be at least two years old. Any less than four years must state its age. White dog must go into the barrel at no more than 62.5% ABV, and the finished product must be bottled at not less than 40% ABV.

One subcategory that is increasingly popular among bourbon aficionados is **Bottled-in-Bond Bourbon**. The Bottled-in-Bond Act of 1897 requires whiskies thus labeled to be produced in a single distilling season (there are two recognized distilling seasons: spring—January to the end of June, and fall—July to the end of December).

It must be made at a single distillery and matured in a U.S. Government bonded warehouse for at least four years and be a minimum 50% ABV. If the whiskey is bottled anywhere other than the distillery of origin, it must be noted on the label. The act also covers other American whiskies, notably rye and corn whiskies, as well as apple brandy.

Tennessee Whiskey—This must be made in Tennessee according to state law. It follows the same rules for bourbon with one additional step known as the Lincoln County Process, which involves dripping the new-make spirit over a vat packed with sugar maple charcoal before going into a barrel. This process smoothes out the whiskey and mellows it. Only one small Tennessee whiskey distiller is exempt.

American Rye Whiskey—This has the same requirements as bourbon, minus the mash bill, when made in the United States. Rye is the most expensive grain to distill—and the most dangerous in inexperienced hands, as it can stick to the inside of stills, causing a catastrophic failure of the still and potentially explosions or fires. Many distillery operators opt not to produce rye whiskey, instead sourcing it from a distillery in Indiana.

American Malt Whiskey—This style is increasingly seen from small distillers in the United States. While U.S. regulations only require 51% malted barley in the mash bill versus 100% for single malt Scotch whisky, there has been a growing movement to both up the requirement for barley to 100% and push for a similar designation for single malt. All other regulations here are similar to bourbon.

America Corn Whiskey—This seems a close cousin to bourbon, and its mash bill requirements and ABV off the still and strength going into the barrel are the same as bourbon, but it's the maturation (or lack thereof) that separates the two. Corn whiskey can be released unaged—there is no requirement for it to touch a barrel, and if it does, it must be matured in either a used or uncharred barrel. Corn whiskey is really about the grain itself.

American Wheat Whiskey—This is another style of whiskey with the same requirements as bourbon, except that the mash bill must be at least 51% wheat.

Now that we've covered the basics, history, and process of making whiskey, let's get to the good stuff. In the next section, we're going to explore some great ways to enjoy whiskey in sixty creative cocktails—some old, some new, and even one with a completely fraudulent history. What all these drinks have in common, though, is that they are delicious. My suggestion is to try them as written first, then play around with the type of whiskey you prefer in each drink. I've offered a couple of caveats where you shouldn't make substitutions, but for the most part, be bold and experiment! Have fun and enjoy yourself. Cheers!

SYRUPS

SIMPLE SYRUP

Add 1 cup of sugar to a small pan. Pour 8 fluid ounces of water into the pan. Heat this over medium heat, stirring occasionally until the sugar dissolves. Remove from the heat and let it cool. Store the syrup in an airtight container in the refrigerator for up to one week.

BROWN SUGAR SIMPLE SYRUP

Add 1 cup of brown sugar to a small pan. Pour 8 fluid ounces of water into the pan. Heat this over medium heat, stirring occasionally until the sugar dissolves. Remove from the heat and let it cool. Store the syrup in an airtight container in the refrigerator for up to one week.

GINGER SYRUP

Add 1 cup of sugar to a small pan. Add 1 thumb-sized piece of peeled and sliced ginger to the pan. Pour 8 fluid ounces of water into the pan. Heat this over medium heat, stirring occasionally until the sugar dissolves. Remove from the heat and let the ginger steep for 20 minutes. Strain out the ginger with a mesh strainer. Store the syrup in an airtight container in the refrigerator for up to one week.

HONEY-GINGER SYRUP

Add 8 fluid ounces of honey to a small pan. Add 1 thumb-sized piece of peeled and sliced ginger to the pan. Pour 8 fluid ounces of water into the pan. Cook over high heat, stirring occasionally until the mixture boils. Reduce the heat to medium and simmer for 5 minutes. Remove from the heat and let the ginger steep for 20 minutes. Strain out the ginger with a mesh strainer. Store the syrup in an airtight container in the refrigerator for up to one week.

MAPLE-SPICED SIMPLE SYRUP

In a small pan, combine 4 fluid ounces of maple syrup, 2 cinnamon sticks, 2 star anise, 5 whole cloves, and 4 fluid ounces of water. Bring to a boil and then turn off the heat. Cover and let stand for at least 30 minutes (or up to overnight), then strain into an airtight, sterilized container. This can be stored in the refrigerator for up to one week.

THE RECIPES

OLD FASHIONED

OLD-FASHIONED

This drink is just that, old-fashioned. When celebrity bartender "Professor" Jerry Thomas wrote the world's first bartenders' guide, *How to Mix Drinks or The Bon Vivant's Companion*, in 1862, his Old-Fashioned recipe called for Holland Gin. By the 1880s, a bartender at the famed Pendennis Club in Louisville, Kentucky, is believed to have popularized a bourbon version, taking it to New York's Waldorf Astoria Hotel, from where it spread to the rest of the world. Whatever its history, this is one of the most important whiskey drinks around. We offer it both ways—the traditional recipe and the modern, post-Prohibition version with muddled fruit. Both have their adherents, so why not try them both?

Ingredients

CLASSIC

2 fluid ounces good bourbon or rye whiskey
½ fluid ounce Simple Syrup (see page 20)
4 dashes of Angostura bitters
a large orange twist and an amarena cherry, to garnish

MODERN

1 sugar cube
6 dashes of Angostura bitters
a large orange twist and an amarena cherry
2 fluid ounces whiskey
2 fluid ounces soda water

Instructions

For the Classic, pour the whiskey into a glass named, appropriately enough, an old-fashioned. Add the Simple Syrup and bitters. Add ice—preferably a single large cube or rock, but the larger the lumps the better. Cut a large orange twist, being careful to only get the skin and not the bitter pith, and express it over the drink with a twisting motion. Drop it in. Garnish with the orange twist and an amarena cherry. For the modern take, place a sugar cube in the glass and sprinkle it with the bitters. Add the orange twist and an amarena cherry and muddle the fruit and sugar cube. Pour in the whiskey and add ice, then top up with soda water. Serve.

MANHATTAN

Not only one of the finest cocktails ever served, this is also one of the most famous. Like many cocktails, the origins of the Manhattan are murky, although some say that it was created in the 1880s at the Manhattan Club for Winston Churchill's mother, Lady Randolph Churchill. This classic combination of whiskey, vermouth, and bitters makes it a foundational cocktail for all bartenders and a great drink for experimenting with different whiskies. Originally rye would have been used, but now bourbon and other whiskies appear in this drink across the globe. Take it a step further and substitute dry vermouth for sweet for a "Dry Manhattan," or use equal parts sweet and dry vermouth for a "Perfect Manhattan." One variation pays tribute to the legendary group of entertainers who put Las Vegas on the map. The "Rat Pack Manhattan" has one ingredient for each member, so in addition to the whiskey, use equal parts sweet and dry vermouth, a dash of Grand Marnier, and 2 or 3 dashes of Angostura bitters. Stir over ice to the sounds of Sammy Davis Jr. and garnish with a cherry, and even an orange twist.

Ingredients
2 fluid ounces whiskey (bourbon or rye are most frequently used, or use Canadian whisky or a blended whiskey)
1 fluid ounce good sweet vermouth
2 dashes of Angostura bitters
an amarena cherry, to garnish

Instructions
Into a cocktail mixing glass, pour the whiskey, sweet vermouth, and bitters. Add some ice and stir with a barspoon until chilled—about 1 minute. Strain into a chilled martini glass and garnish with an amarena cherry.

WELCOME TO Manhattan

HOTEL

Ballantine's

— FINEST —

BLENDED SCOTCH WHISKY

GEORGE BALLANTINE AND SON
DUMBARTON, G82 2SS, SCOTLAND
PRODUCT OF SCOTLAND

70cl e   40%vol

ROB ROY

Also occasionally referred to as a "Scotch whisky Manhattan," this is the Manhattan's close relative in the cocktail world. It is reputed to have been originally created in 1894 at the Waldorf Astoria Hotel, in New York City, for the premiere of an operetta called, obviously enough, *Rob Roy*, which was based on the Scottish outlaw and folk hero. This cocktail works best with a blended Scotch whisky that has a smoky character, but don't be afraid to play around with your favorite single malt here, too.

Ingredients
2 fluid ounces blended Scotch whisky
1 fluid ounce good sweet vermouth
2 dashes of Angostura bitters
an amarena cherry, to garnish

Instructions
Pour the whisky, sweet vermouth, and bitters into a cocktail mixing glass. Add some ice and stir with a barspoon until chilled—about 1 minute. Strain into a chilled martini glass and garnish with an amarena cherry.

CINNAMANHATTAN

This was created by San Francisco bartender Sierra Zimei in 2008. By adding Grand Marnier and bitters to a high-rye bourbon, it showcases some delicious cinnamon and spice notes in a drink that is also very easy to prepare. The Cinnamanhattan is a riff on the classic Manhattan and provides a good example for home mixologists on how a minor substitution to a cocktail can create something entirely new and different.

Ingredients
2½ fluid ounces high-rye bourbon
½ fluid ounce Grand Marnier
5 dashes of Angostura bitters
a cinnamon stick and dried cherries
on a cocktail pick, to garnish

Instructions
Add the bourbon, Grand Marnier, and Angostura bitters to a mixing glass. Add some ice and stir for 1 minute, then strain into a martini glass. Garnish with a cinnamon stick and dried cherries on a cocktail pick.

Marnier-Lapostolle

CORDON ROUGE

Maison Fondée en 1827

Grand Marnier

LIQUEUR
ORANGE & COGNAC

PARIS-FRANCE

BROOKLYN

BROOKLYN

While this cocktail may be less well known than the more uptown Manhattan, just because it has fallen into a bit of post-Prohibition obscurity doesn't mean it should be ignored. If you enjoy cocktails that are brown, bitter, and stirred, then this is the drink for you. You may occasionally spot this cocktail on the menu at a mixology-focused bar, as it is adored by many bartenders in that world—but don't order one of these at a local tavern and expect anything more than a blank stare from the barkeep. That said, the best way to enjoy the Brooklyn is prepared by your own hands.

Ingredients
2 fluid ounces rye whiskey
1 fluid ounce dry vermouth
½ fluid ounce Picon Amer (substitute Ramazzotti Amaro liqueur if need be)
½ fluid ounce maraschino liqueur
4 dashes of orange bitters
a large orange twist, to garnish

Instructions
Pour the rye whiskey, dry vermouth, Picon Amer, maraschino liqueur, and orange bitters into a mixing glass. Add some ice and stir for 1 minute. Strain into a chilled coupe or martini glass and garnish with a large orange twist.

JOHN COLLINS

Most likely descended from the late 19th-century punch style of cocktail, this drink would have originally included water, a spirit, fruit, sugar, and spices. At that time, punches would have been made in large punch bowls, but the John Collins offers a more manageable individual serving. Light and refreshing, this is the whiskey-based cousin of the better-known, gin-based Tom Collins. The John Collins is a perfect vehicle for experimenting with different whiskies; bourbon, Canadian whisky, and Irish whiskey are all ideal choices, but feel free to find your own perfect match.

Ingredients
1 ½ fluid ounces whiskey (bourbon is traditional)
¾ fluid ounce freshly squeezed lemon juice
¾ fluid ounce Simple Syrup (see page 20)
4 fluid ounces soda water
a lemon slice and cherry, to garnish

Instructions
Half fill a cocktail shaker with ice. Pour in the whiskey, lemon juice, and Simple Syrup, then shake vigorously for 1 minute. Strain into a highball glass filled with fresh ice cubes. Top with soda water and garnish with a lemon slice and cherry.

WHISKEY HIGHBALL

This cocktail is making a comeback, which certainly isn't surprising. A refreshing combination of whiskey, ice, and soda water or ginger ale, this one is easy to make and easy to drink. It's the perfect cocktail for a Monday evening after a rough day at work when you want something both simple and delicious. For a more exacting take on the Highball, we go to Japan, where the Mizuwari (meaning "mixed with water") has a ritual all its own. Fill a glass with whiskey (Japanese whisky preferred) and ice, then stir 13½ times (slowly). Top up the drink with ice again and add sparkling water. Now stir 3½ more times to incorporate everything and serve. Just don't forget what your count is on the stirs or you'll ruin not only your Mizuwari but also lose face for being unable to count to seventeen while making a drink.

Ingredients
2 fluid ounces whiskey
4 fluid ounces soda water or ginger ale

Instructions
Pour the whiskey into a highball glass. Add some fresh ice cubes and top with soda water or ginger ale.

LOMO

Modern Highball-style drinks are a trend right now, and James Ault from Dig-A-Pony in Portland, Oregon is on point with the Lomo, a cocktail Highball mixing bourbon with ginger drinking vinegar, yellow chartreuse, orange bitters, and soda water. The trendy drinking vinegar adds a bit of Asian flair to this drink and the result is a complex Highball that is eminently quaffable. Add the complex herbal notes of the yellow chartreuse, which contributes just enough sweetness to mellow the bite of the drinking vinegar and enhances the bourbon, and this is a cocktail you won't soon forget.

Ingredients

1 ½ fluid ounces bourbon
½ fluid ounce yellow chartreuse
¾ fluid ounce ginger drinking vinegar
2 dashes of orange bitters
soda water, to top up
fresh basil leaves and a flamed orange peel (see page 60), to garnish

Instructions

Combine the bourbon, yellow charteuse, drinking vinegar, and orange bitters in a highball glass. Add some fresh ice cubes and top up with the soda water. Stir gently to incorporate and garnish with fresh basil leaves and a flamed orange peel.

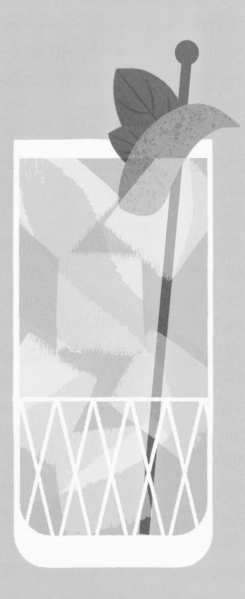

Blanton's
THE ORIGINAL
SINGLE BARREL
BOURBON WHISKEY

SODA
WATER

Bourbon Whiskey dumped on 4-2009 from Barrel No 300
Stored in Warehouse H on Rick No 38
Traditionally selected filtered and bottled by hand at 93 Proof

RAIGHT BOURBON WHISKEY   46% ALC/VOL (93 PROOF)

WHISKEY RICKEY

This is a refreshing long drink that eschews sugar for a tart combination of whiskey, lime, and soda water. This drink was originally created by a bartender named George A. Williamson at Shoomaker's Bar in Washington, D.C., in the 1880s. The original recipe calls for bourbon, although any whiskey will work well in this drink. Ironically, it wasn't until gin was substituted for bourbon about ten years after this drink's creation that the Rickey took off in popularity. The large majority of Rickeys are still ordered with gin, but try this with your favorite whiskey and enjoy a tipple that 19th-century U.S. Congressmen would have sipped during the warm-weather months in the capital.

Ingredients
2 fluid ounces bourbon or whiskey of choice
soda water, to top up
½ lime, for squeezing and garnish

Instructions
Fill a highball glass with ice, add the whiskey, and top up with soda water. Squeeze the ½ lime into the drink and drop in the lime shell as a garnish.

BOBBY BURNS

Named after the great Scottish poet Robert Burns, whose poem *Address to a Haggis* is one of his best-known pieces of writing and a staple at Burns Night (January 25) whisky celebrations the world over, this three-ingredient cocktail combines Scotch whisky with sweet vermouth and Benedictine liqueur. While it may seem simple, the end result is a cocktail with a depth and complexity far beyond these three separate ingredients. Don't wait until Burns Night to discover this one, though; the Bobby Burns also makes a great accompaniment to a steak dinner.

Ingredients
1 fluid ounce blended Scotch whisky
½ fluid ounce Benedictine liqueur
1 fluid ounce sweet vermouth
a lemon twist, to garnish

Instructions
Pour the blended Scotch, Benedictine, and sweet vermouth into a mixing glass. Add ice and stir for 1 minute. Strain into a chilled coupe or martini glass and garnish with a lemon twist.

J&B
RARE
A BLEND OF THE PUREST
OLD SCOTCH WHISKIES
JUSTERINI & BROOKS
St James's Street London S.W.
KING GEORGE III
PRODUCED AND BOTTLED IN SCOTLAND
70cl e
40% vol

BOURBON DAISY

This is one of the Daisy category of cocktails that has expanded beyond its original grouping to become a bit of an amorphous drink. This particular version is a nod to the 19th-century, classic Daisy style, although you'll often find modern versions of this drink to be little more than a Whiskey Sour with added soda water. You could easily make this version a long drink by doing just that, but the real charm of this cocktail is the interplay between whiskey and yellow chartreuse, an herbal liqueur made by Carthusian monks in France. Just about any nonpeated whiskey will work well here—the question is simply which one works best for your palate.

Ingredients
2 fluid ounces whiskey
¾ fluid ounce freshly squeezed lemon juice
½ fluid ounce grenadine
½ fluid ounce yellow chartreuse

Instructions
Pour the whiskey, lemon juice, and grenadine into a mixing glass. Add some ice and stir for 1 minute. Strain into a chilled coupe or martini glass. Float the yellow chartreuse on top of the drink by pouring it over the back of a barspoon onto the surface of the cocktail and serve.

SCOFFLAW

This drink wins the award for "Best Name for a Cocktail," as it was developed during Prohibition and the name literally means "a person who drinks illegally." Debuting at the famous Harry's New York Bar in Paris in 1924, which would have been filled with American celebrities traveling overseas for cocktails and fun, this mixture of lemon, whiskey, and vermouth appears in a number of drinks from this time. Harry's Bar is still open in Paris, and it remains a throwback to those glory days. The Scofflaw works best with rye or bourbon. A word of warning: be careful of choosing another style of whiskey for this drink; substitutes generally don't work well. Some bartenders prefer to swap lime juice for lemon, but that is up to individual tastes.

Ingredients
2 fluid ounces rye whiskey or bourbon
1 fluid ounce dry vermouth
¼ fluid ounce freshly squeezed lemon juice
½ fluid ounce grenadine
2 dashes of orange bitters

Instructions
Half fill a cocktail shaker with ice. Pour in the whiskey, vermouth, lemon juice, grenadine, and bitters and shake vigorously for 60 seconds. Strain into a coupe or martini glass and serve.

PAPER PLANE

Created by New York bartender Sam Ross, this modern cocktail classic is stunningly beautiful and refreshing and complex, making it the perfect aperitif. It is easy to make, simply being equal parts of each ingredient combined, and can be pre-batched for cocktail parties—just increase the ingredients to make however many drinks you need, then pour the cocktail into a shaker, one batch at a time, with some ice, shake and strain. This classic drink works best with bourbon.

Ingredients
¾ fluid ounce bourbon
¾ fluid ounce Aperol
¾ fluid ounce Amaro Nonino
¾ fluid ounce freshly squeezed lemon juice
a lemon twist, to garnish

Instructions
Half fill a cocktail shaker with ice. Pour in the bourbon, Aperol, Amaro Nonino, and lemon juice, then shake vigorously for 1 minute. Strain into a martini glass or coupe. Garnish with a lemon twist.

BLOOD AND SAND

This cocktail gets its name from the eponymous 1922 bullfighting film starring Rudolph Valentino. The recipe for this drink first appeared in print in *The Savoy Cocktail Book* in 1930. Originally, it would have been made with blood orange juice (much more common in Europe than in the United States). The red color of the juice was supposed to call to mind the blood of the bulls in the movie, and while this is considered one of Valentino's finest performances, the movie itself opened to less than enthusiastic reviews. This is also one of the few classic cocktails to use Cherry Heering, a Danish cherry brandy that is matured for three years before being bottled.

Ingredients
¾ fluid ounce blended Scotch whisky
¾ fluid ounce Cherry Heering liqueur
¾ fluid ounce sweet vermouth
¾ fluid ounce freshly squeezed orange
juice (blood orange, if possible)
a large orange twist, to garnish

Instructions
Half fill a cocktail shaker with ice. Pour in the whisky, Cherry Heering, sweet vermouth, and orange juice and shake vigorously for 1 minute. Strain into a coupe or martini glass and garnish with a large orange twist expressed over the drink.

BOULEVARDIER

If you haven't heard of the Boulevardier, it is the cousin of the better-known gin-based cocktail, the Negroni. Originally appearing in American-expat and celebrity bartender Harry MacElhone's 1927 cocktail book *Barflies and Cocktails*, it is mentioned as the signature drink of one Erskine Gwynne, socialite and editor of the Paris-based journal, *The Boulevardier*. A deceptively simple drink, many recipes for the Boulevardier will merely call for equal parts whiskey, Campari, and sweet vermouth for simplicity, but increasing the proportion of whiskey results in a better-balanced cocktail. Stick to rye whiskey or a high rye-content bourbon for best results.

Ingredients
1½ fluid ounces rye whiskey or bourbon
1 fluid ounce sweet vermouth
1 fluid ounce Campari
an orange twist, to garnish

Instructions
Pour the whiskey or bourbon, sweet vermouth, and Campari into a mixing glass. Add some ice and stir with a barspoon until chilled—about 1 minute. Strain into a chilled martini glass and garnish with an orange twist expressed over the surface of the drink.

OLD PAL

Today this cocktail is made with rye whiskey, but the original version would have used Canadian whisky. The Old Pal is constructed in a similar way to the gin-based Negroni, but dry vermouth is substituted for sweet and the rye for gin. This classic drink also dates back to Harry MacElhone's 1927 book, *Barflies and Cocktails*, and it makes a drier and smoother change of pace from the usual Manhattans and Boulevardiers.

Ingredients
1 fluid ounce rye whiskey
1 fluid ounce dry vermouth
1 fluid ounce Campari
a lemon or orange twist, to garnish

Instructions
Pour the rye whiskey, dry vermouth, and Campari into a mixing glass. Add some ice and stir for 1 minute. Strain into a chilled coupe or martini glass and garnish with a lemon or orange twist.

PENICILLIN

The aptly named Penicillin is a modern classic crafted by bartender Sam Ross. Created in 2005, the Penicillin mixes Scotch whisky with honey, ginger, and lemon to create one of the best and most popular Scotch-based drinks of modern times. Walk into a mixology bar in Hong Kong, London, Seattle, or anywhere in between, sidle up to the bar, order a Penicillin, and enjoy the drink that has gone viral.

Ingredients
2 fluid ounces blended Scotch whisky
¾ fluid ounce Honey-Ginger Syrup (see page 20)
¾ fluid ounce freshly squeezed lemon juice
¼ fluid ounce Islay single malt Scotch whisky
grated candied ginger, to garnish

Instructions
Pour the blended Scotch whisky, Honey-Ginger Syrup, lemon juice, and Islay whisky into a mixing glass. Add some ice and stir for 1 minute. Strain into a chilled coupe glass and garnish with a little candied ginger on a cocktail pick.

SUFFERING BASTARD

The Suffering Bastard is perhaps the strangest cocktail in this book. Created in the 1940s by Joe Scialom at the Long Bar at the Shepheard's Hotel in Cairo, Egypt (not exactly a hotbed of mixology), this potent mixture of bourbon, gin, lime juice, bitters, and ginger ale was originally designed as a hangover cure. The hotel was a hangout for British army officers during World War II, and enough of them had such bad hangovers that they would decide to drink them off (not recommended except in war zones). Thus this cocktail became the signature drink.

Ingredients
1 fluid ounce bourbon
1 fluid ounce gin
1 fluid ounce freshly squeezed lime juice
1 dash of Angostura bitters
4 fluid ounces ginger ale
an orange slice and a sprig of fresh mint, to garnish

Instructions
Pour the bourbon, gin, lime juice, and Angostura bitters into a mixing glass. Add some ice and stir for 1 minute. Strain into an old-fashioned glass filled with fresh ice cubes, top with ginger ale, and garnish with an orange slice and a sprig of mint.

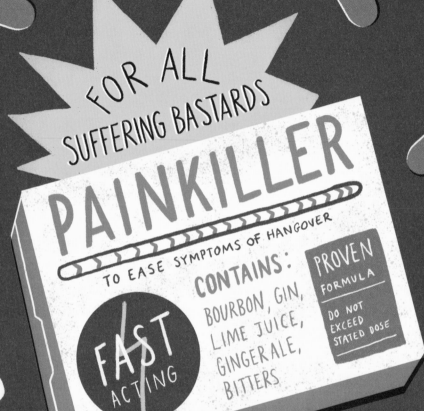

PRESBYTERIAN

Otherwise known as "Press" for short, this cocktail is a
bar staple—both for its simplicity and its refreshing
taste. It is a close cousin of the Highball for its
combination of whiskey, soda water, and ginger ale.
Originally created in the 1890s, this drink is actually
named after the Presbyterian Church, which originated
primarily in Scotland, and the original recipe for this
drink called for Scotch whisky—hence the name. Today,
any whiskey is acceptable, so feel free to experiment.

Ingredients
1 ½ fluid ounces whiskey
2 fluid ounces soda water
2 fluid ounces ginger ale
a lemon wedge, to garnish

Instructions
Fill a highball glass with fresh ice cubes and pour in the whiskey.
Top with soda and ginger ale and garnish with a lemon wedge.

JOHN JONES

This cocktail, created by Jacob Grier—Portland, Oregon's magic enthusiast and bartender—falls into the bitter and stirred style of whiskey drinks by featuring both sweet vermouth and an Italian amaro to play with the spice notes in the rye whiskey base. The flamed orange peel adds just enough brightness to the drink, and let's be frank—flaming an orange peel adds a certain showmanship that can't fail to impress your guests.

Ingredients
2 fluid ounces 100% proof rye whiskey
¾ fluid ounce Carpano Antica Formula
¾ fluid ounce Amaro Ramazzotti
a flamed orange twist, to garnish (see below)

Instructions
Combine the rye whiskey, Carpano Antica, and Amaro Ramazzotti in a cocktail shaker. Add some ice and shake vigorously. Strain over fresh ice cubes and garnish with a flamed orange twist. Serve immediately.

How to flame an orange twist: First cut a wide piece of peel without any pith (a Y-shaped vegetable peeler helps). Keeping the skin between your thumb and forefinger, begin to heat the peel with a lighter. After a few seconds of warming, squeeze the zest above the surface of the drink to create a large flame.

ESTᴰ 1978
RUSTY'S
BLENDED SCOTCH WHISKY

PRODUCT OF SCOTLAND

ORIGINAL

RUSTY NAIL

That classic mix of Scotch whisky and Drambuie (a Scotch whisky-based liqueur flavored with honey and herbs and associated with Bonnie Prince Charlie) has also lent its name to an entire category of drink preparation: Nail-style drinks. While the origins of the Rusty Nail are a bit murky, the best theory is that it was created at New York's Club 21, where bartenders could take the edge off rougher spirits often found during Prohibition by adding the sweetness of Drambuie. No matter its origin, the Rusty Nail continues to have legions of fans and is a delightful Scotch cocktail. No substitutions either on Scotch whisky or the Drambuie, please.

Ingredients
1 fluid ounce blended Scotch whisky
1 fluid ounce Drambuie

Instructions
Pour the whisky and Drambuie into a rocks glass, add a little fresh ice, then stir gently to incorporate.

THE GODFATHER

A mixture of Scotch whisky and amaretto in what bartenders refer to as a Nail-style drink—into which any combination of a base spirit (in this case, Scotch) and sweetener (amaretto) fall. This recipe calls for a 1–1 ratio of Scotch to amaretto, but feel free to play with the proportions as you like. This is a drink where a big, bold Scotch whisky works best, as the sweetness of the amaretto takes things down a notch and civilizes even the most uncouth of whiskies in your cabinet. Master this drink, then take this general idea and apply it to a number of different liqueurs and create all kinds of "nails" of your own.

Ingredients
1 ½ fluid ounces Scotch whisky
1 ½ fluid ounces amaretto

Instructions
Add the whisky and amaretto to a rocks glass. Add some fresh ice cubes and stir gently to incorporate. Serve.

SAZERAC

One of New Orleans's many contributions to cocktail culture, the Sazerac was originally made with French cognac in the 1850s. Named after Sazerac de Forge et Fils, a then-popular cognac brand, it used a local bitters produced by Antoine Amédée Peychaud—Peychaud's bitters. By the 1870s, due to cognac shortages after the phylloxera infestation in France's vineyards, rye whiskey was substituted and has since become the drink's base ingredient. The Sazerac has been the official cocktail of New Orleans since 2008. While it's a great drink to sip in the Big Easy, you can also easily replicate it at home. Stick with rye whiskey here, as other whiskies make poor substitutes. If you are feeling experimental, try the original recipe with a VSOP-level cognac instead of rye whiskey.

Ingredients
1 sugar cube
4 dashes of Peychaud's bitters
¼ fluid ounce water
1 ½ fluid ounces rye whiskey
¼ fluid ounce absinthe
a large lemon twist, to garnish

Instructions
Take two old-fashioned glasses. Fill the first with ice and set it aside to chill. In the second, combine a sugar cube with the bitters and water, and gently muddle to dissolve the sugar. Pour in the rye whiskey, add some ice, and stir for 30 seconds. Next, dump the ice from the first glass and pour in the absinthe, swirling it to coat the inside of the glass. Discard any extra absinthe in the bottom of the glass. Strain the whiskey mixture into the absinthe-rinsed glass. Express a large lemon twist over the top of the drink, rubbing it around the inside rim of the glass to maximize the flavor, then discard it. Serve.

TORONTO

This is not a drink for amateurs. Originally, Canadian whisky was used (although rye is more common today) and combined with Fernet (a very bitter type of Italian amaro), bitters, and just a touch of sugar. This cocktail originally appeared in the 1922 cocktail book *Cocktails: How to Mix Them*, by London barman Robert Vermeire, who noted that this drink was "much appreciated" by Canadians from Toronto. Given that the province of Ontario had a prohibition on alcohol from 1916 until 1927, it is safe to assume that this drink was most likely created in London and favored by traveling Canadians.

Ingredients
2 fluid ounces rye whiskey (or Canadian whisky, to be authentic)
¼ fluid ounce Fernet-Branca
¼ fluid ounce Simple Syrup (see page 20)
2 dashes of Angostura bitters
a large orange twist, to garnish

Instructions
Pour the rye whiskey, Fernet-Branca, Simple Syrup, and Angostura bitters into a mixing glass. Add some ice and stir for 1 minute. Strain into a chilled martini or old-fashioned glass and garnish with a large orange twist.

COOPER'S COCKTAIL

A bartender in Seattle by way of Canada, Jamie Boudreau, proprietor of Canon in the Emerald City, is the creator of this drink. While the Toronto (see page 68) is an older style of a whiskey-and-Fernet cocktail, with the Cooper's, Boudreau has tempered the bitterness inherent in the amaro with elderflower liqueur and allowed both the Fernet and the elderflower to complement the spice notes in the rye whiskey. The result is a modern classic and one that's worth creating at home.

Ingredients
2 fluid ounces rye whiskey
¾ fluid ounce elderflower liqueur
¼ fluid ounce Fernet-Branca
an orange twist, to garnish

Instructions
Pour the rye whiskey, elderflower liqueur, and Fernet-Branca into a mixing glass. Add some ice and stir for 1 minute. Strain into a chilled coupe or martini glass and garnish with an orange twist.

OLD BAY RIDGE

This creation comes from modern cocktail historian David Wondrich, but it tastes like a cocktail that would have originated in the 1920s. Rye whiskey shares the stage with aquavit, a Scandinavian spirit similar to vodka that is spiced with caraway or dill. This recipe calls for Linie Aquavit, which is matured at sea, making a transequatorial trip from Norway to Australia and back, before being bottled. It is notoriously tough to mix cocktails with aquavit, but this is an amazing cocktail and one worth investing in this unique spirit.

Ingredients
1 sugar cube
2 dashes of Angostura bitters
1 fluid ounce rye whiskey
1 fluid ounce Linie Aquavit

Instructions
Start by muddling the sugar cube, Angostura bitters, rye whiskey, and aquavit in a mixing glass. Next add some ice and stir to combine the flavors. Strain into an old-fashioned glass filled with fresh ice cubes.

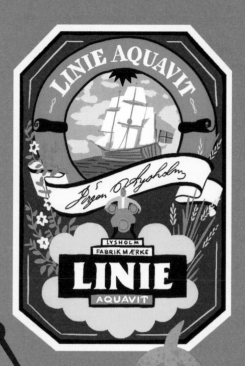

Welcome to KENTUCKY

KENTUCKY MULE

This cocktail is a member of the family of drinks known as mules or bucks, of which the most famous is the vodka-based Moscow Mule, created in the 1940s at Hollywood's famous Cock 'n' Bull. However, mules and bucks have been around for much longer. While the origin of these drinks is unclear, legend has it that adding a spirit such as whiskey to ginger beer gave the drink a "kick," hence the name. Obviously, bourbon is the classic call here, but rye whiskey will up the spiciness factor a bit, while an American blended whiskey is a perfectly fine choice for a lighter, smoother option. The choice is yours.

Ingredients
2 fluid ounces bourbon
4 fluid ounces ginger beer
a lime wedge, to garnish

Instructions
Pour the bourbon into a copper mug. Add fresh ice cubes, then fill to the brim with ginger beer. Garnish with a lime wedge.

REMEMBER THE MAINE

"Remember the Maine" was a rallying cry for the Spanish–American War in 1898 that led to Cuban independence. While few people remember the sinking of the *USS Maine* in Havana harbor, the drink is a reminder of that historic time, and it uses good American rye whiskey in a patriotic nod. The drink first appeared in Charles Baker's 1939 cocktail book, *The Gentleman's Companion: Being an Exotic Drinking Book Or, Around the World with Jigger, Beaker, and Flask*. Think of this as a Manhattan cocktail modified with a bit of Cherry Heering and absinthe. The key to this drink is using rye whiskey only (no substitutions, please!) and going easy on the absinthe. A little absinthe goes a long way, and too much will quickly tip this cocktail from delicious to unpleasant.

Ingredients
2 fluid ounces rye whiskey
¾ fluid ounce sweet vermouth
¼ teaspoon absinthe
2 teaspoons Cherry Heering liqueur
a cherry, to garnish

Instructions
Pour the rye whiskey, sweet vermouth, absinthe, and Cherry Heering into a mixing glass. Add ice and mix for 6 seconds. Strain into a chilled coupe glass and garnish with a cherry.

RST PUBLISHING

1939

THE GENTLEMAN'S COMPANION

VOL.1
BEING AN EXOTIC
COOKERY BOOK

VOL.2
BEING AN EXOTIC
DRINKING BOOK

CHARLES H.
BAKER, JR.

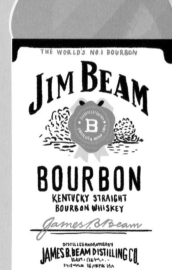

CHATHAM ARTILLERY PUNCH

(Serves 45 x 4-fluid-ounce servings)

This is a throwback to the 1800s, and while many drinks from that era just don't hold up for modern palates, the Chatham Artillery Punch remains as relevant as ever. Essentially just a simple combination of whiskey, cognac, rum, and sparkling wine with a bit of sugar and lemon thrown in for good measure, this punch will serve an entire military regiment and then some, between the volume of drinks and the sheer strength of each serving. This drink is best served in small portions.

Ingredients
12 lemons
2¼ cups superfine sugar
1 bottle cognac
1 bottle bourbon
1 bottle dark rum
3 bottles sparkling wine

Instructions
Using a Y-shaped vegetable peeler, peel all the lemons, leaving the white pith behind. Combine the peels and sugar in a bowl and muddle together to combine, then set aside to rest for 2 hours.

Juice enough lemons to obtain 16 fluid ounces of lemon juice, then pour this over the peels and sugar mixture. Add 4 fluid ounces of water, strain off the peels and reserve the lemon juice/sugar mixture. Fill a punch bowl with cracked ice and pour in all the bottles of whiskey, rum, and wine, plus the sugar and lemon mixture. Stir to combine and serve in small punch glasses.

FEZ MEDINA

Denver Colorado's Ky Belk is one of the most talented bartenders in America today. A winner of numerous awards for his bartending, Belk juggles running multiple beverage programs at some of Denver's top restaurants and bars. With the Fez Medina, rye whiskey is combined with Aperol, amaro, and orange bitters to highlight the spice notes and orange undertones in the rye whiskey. This is a deceptively simple drink that delivers layer upon layer of flavor.

Ingredients
1 ½ fluid ounces rye whiskey
¾ fluid ounce Amaro CioCiaro
½ fluid ounce Aperol
3 dashes of orange bitters
a dehydrated orange slice, to garnish

Instructions
Add the rye whiskey, amaro, Aperol, and orange bitters to a mixing glass. Add some ice and stir for 1 minute. Strain into an old-fashioned glass and garnish with a dehydrated orange slice.

W.D.G ORIGINAL

RUM

· SMALL BATCH ·

Dark

70cle   40% vol

AGED IN OAK
BARRELS
DISTILLED FROM
SUGAR CANE MOLASSES

M.E
OK

PORTO

Niepoort

SINCE 1848

RUBY
DUM

SUBURBAN

This drink dates from the golden age of 19th-century cocktails. This heady mix of rye whiskey, rum, and port wine is a veritable greatest-hits compilation of favored beverages from that era, so it makes sense that someone decided to combine all three. This drink was originally created by bartenders at the Waldorf Astoria Hotel in New York City for a racehorse owner who had a horse running in the Suburban Handicap at Brooklyn's Sheepshead Bay Race Track.

Ingredients
1 ½ fluid ounces rye whiskey
½ fluid ounce dark rum
½ fluid ounce ruby port
1 dash of Angostura bitters
1 dash of orange bitters
an orange twist, to garnish

Instructions
Pour the rye whiskey, dark rum, ruby port, and both bitters into a mixing glass. Add some ice and stir for 1 minute. Strain into a chilled coupe and garnish with an orange twist.

WHISKEY BRAMBLE

This is a variation on a gin-based drink created in 1980 by legendary London barkeep Dick Bradsell at Fred's Club, in London's Soho district. While gin is wonderful here, whiskey (Irish whiskey in particular) is a natural pairing with both lemon and crème de mûre (or blackberry brandy), and the results for this version may be even better than the original. Bradsell said that childhood berry-picking trips on the Isle of Wight inspired this drink, and the name is a nod to those blackberry bushes, otherwise known as brambles.

Ingredients

2 fluid ounces bourbon or Irish whiskey
¾ fluid ounce freshly squeezed lemon juice
¼ fluid ounce Simple Syrup (see page 20)
½ fluid ounce crème de mûre (blackberry brandy)
a few blackberries and a lemon wheel, to garnish

Instructions

Half fill a cocktail shaker with ice. Pour in the bourbon or whiskey, lemon juice, and Simple Syrup, shake vigorously and strain into an old-fashioned glass filled with crushed ice. Drizzle crème de mûre over the top of the drink, then garnish with blackberries and a lemon wheel.

MINT JULEP

A symbol of the American South, the Mint Julep is inextricably linked to the Kentucky Derby horse race, where it has been the official drink since 1938. Amazingly, up to 120,000 juleps are consumed at Churchill Downs over Derby weekend every year. The word "julep" is descended from the Arabic drink "julab," which is made with water and rose petals. The modern julep dates back to the 1700s, and the silver or pewter julep cup is key to this drink. Glass is an insulator, so a proper julep cup will get icy on the outside while it sits. Spearmint is the go-to mint in the South, although peppermint will also work in a pinch. The julep is a rare drink that actually gets better as it sits, so try your hand at one of these on a warm summer day, then sit back and relax, sipping slowly as the world whizzes by.

Ingredients
a large bunch of mint sprigs
½ fluid ounce Simple Syrup (see page 20)
2 fluid ounces bourbon

Instructions
In the bottom of a julep cup, add 8–10 mint leaves, stripped from the bunch, and half the Simple Syrup. Gently muddle the mint in the Simple Syrup, being careful not to bruise the leaves. Fill the julep cup with crushed ice, mounding it over the top and creating a look reminiscent of a snow cone. Slowly pour the bourbon over the top of the ice, followed by the remaining Simple Syrup. Next, take the remaining bunch of mint sprigs and give them a good spank between your hands to release the essential oils. Place these into the ice as a garnish, along with a short (paper) straw so that the aromas of the drink can be better enjoyed.

BOURBON SMASH

A close cousin of the Mint Julep, the Bourbon Smash is enhanced with a slightly different preparation and the addition of lemon juice. The resulting cocktail combines the mint of a julep with the lemon of a sour, creating a happy medium of both. This cocktail takes well to freshly muddled fruit (think berries in particular) as an additional alternative. The Smash is a drink that deserves more attention than it currently gets and is perfect as a warm-weather cocktail.

Ingredients
8–10 mint leaves, plus a sprig to garnish
½ fluid ounce Simple Syrup (see page 20)
2 fluid ounces bourbon
¾ fluid ounce freshly squeezed lemon juice

Instructions
Place the mint leaves at the bottom of a cocktail shaker. Add the Simple Syrup and gently muddle the mint leaves. Add some ice cubes, and pour in the bourbon and lemon juice. Shake vigorously and strain into an old-fashioned glass filled with fresh ice cubes. Garnish with a sprig of freshly spanked mint.

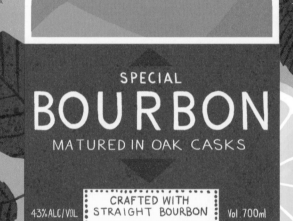

SPECIAL
BOURBON
MATURED IN OAK CASKS

CRAFTED WITH
STRAIGHT BOURBON

43% ALC/VOL

Vol. 700ml

DERBY

The Derby cocktail is served by bartenders in a couple of variations, but this version with sweet vermouth, orange curaçao, and lime juice is the real classic. Originally created by tiki legend "Trader Vic" Bergeron, this version of the Derby produces a drink with herbal overtones offset by the tartness of the lime. Tiki fans beware: despite the link with Trader Vic, this isn't a tiki drink. Instead it is a serious whiskey drink that showcases Trader Vic's ability to go "off brand" and create classic cocktails without an island vibe.

Ingredients
1 fluid ounce whiskey
½ fluid ounce sweet vermouth
½ fluid ounce orange curaçao
¾ fluid ounce freshly squeezed lime juice
a lime wedge and mint leaves, to garnish

Instructions
Pour the whiskey, sweet vermouth, orange curaçao, and lime juice into a cocktail shaker along with some ice. Shake vigorously and strain into a martini glass. Garnish with a lime wedge and mint leaves.

FROZEN THAI WHISKEY COKE

This cocktail contains both Thai whiskey and bourbon, but only one of those ingredients is actually whiskey . . . Thai whiskey is actually closer to a rum, as it is made from 95% sugar or molasses and 5% rice, which is then flavored with local herbs and spices for a spirit that is uniquely Thai. This delicious drink from mixologist Ky Belk is a great excuse to break out your blender on a warm day and whip up this refreshing frozen drink.

Ingredients
1 fluid ounce Mekhong Thai whiskey
1 fluid ounce bottled-in-bond bourbon
¼ fluid ounce freshly squeezed lime juice
1 barspoon ginger juice (shop-bought or home-juice—alternatively, swap for ginger beer)
4 fluid ounces cola

Instructions
If juicing your own ginger, peel it first. Pour both whiskies, the lime juice, ginger juice, and cola into a blender along with one giant scoop of ice. Blend until combined, then pour into whatever glass you may have on hand that looks like it might fit!

SEELBACH

This cocktail hails from Louisville, Kentucky, where it was created at the Seelbach Hotel in the 1800s. Oh wait, no, forget that . . . It was actually a Kentucky bartender who created it in the 1990s and then lied about the origins of the drink for twenty years, before eventually confessing. The bartender claimed that the drink was discovered on an old menu at the hotel, but he finally admitted that he concocted the story because it sounded better. (The bar world isn't known for letting truth stand in the way of a good story.) Regardless, the Seelbach is a great drink with echoes back to the classics. Make one of these and raise a toast to one of the greatest frauds the cocktail world has ever seen.

Ingredients
1 fluid ounce bourbon
½ fluid ounce Cointreau
6 dashes each of Angostura and Peychaud's bitters
sparkling wine, to top up
a lemon twist, to garnish

Instructions
Pour the bourbon, Cointreau, and bitters into a mixing glass. Add some ice and stir for 1 minute. Strain into a champagne flute and top up with sparkling wine. Garnish with a lemon twist.

DUCK FART

No cocktail book is complete without a reference to flatulence, and the Duck Fart is the only whiskey drink that meets the criteria, so here it is. It was created at the Peanut Farm in Anchorage, Alaska, in the 1990s during a time when all the good names for cocktails were taken. Great drink, lousy name. To pay homage to the era that spawned this unfortunately titled drink, some bartenders don't even bother layering this pousse-café-style drink with a barspoon and instead just use a maraschino cherry to build up the spirits. Why not try this yourself?

Ingredients
½ fluid ounce coffee liqueur
½ fluid ounce Irish cream liqueur, such as Bailey's
½ fluid ounce whiskey

Instructions
Using the back of a barspoon to pour over, layer the drink into a shot glass. Start with the coffee liqueur, followed by the Irish cream, and then finish with the whiskey on top.

IRISH

SHOT

D
R
O
P

GUINNESS

ESTᴰ 1759

IRISH DROP SHOT

This is a simple, tasty, and very, very Irish cocktail. It is a drink for socializing and partying, not for putting into a snifter to discuss its many qualities. One word of warning, though—because this drink goes down so easily, some people won't pay attention to their consumption and can overdo it quickly. Pace yourself with a full glass of water or other nonalcoholic beverage in between rounds and be aware that this one can sneak up on you pretty quickly.

St. Patrick's Day is the most famous day to consume this drink in the United States, but it's an appropriate order any time one wants to get the party started!

Ingredients
¾ fluid ounce Irish whiskey
¾ fluid ounce Bailey's Irish Cream
8 fluid ounces Guinness Irish Stout

Instructions
In a shot glass, combine the Irish whiskey and Irish Cream. Pour the Guinness into a pint glass, then drop the shot glass into the beer and consume immediately.

BOILERMAKER

This is the kind of drink one expects dockworkers and other salt-of-the-earth types to drink in the morning for breakfast right after a tough night's work. However, any combination of a beer and a shot of whiskey is actually a Boilermaker—it's up to you how you drink it.

A classic light lager is the traditional choice for the Boilermaker.

Ingredients
2 fluid ounces whiskey
16 fluid ounces beer (a classic light lager)

Instructions
There are two options here.
Option 1: drop a shot of whiskey into a glass of beer and drink immediately; or option 2: pour the whiskey and beer into separate glasses and alternate sips of each.

TOMATO

Juice

SAUCE

SAUCE CO.
PREMIUM SAUCES SINCE
1938

WORCESTERSHIRE
SAUCE

McILHENNY CO
AVERY ISLAND
L.A
TABASCO
BRAND
PEPPER SAUCE

CELERY
SALT

SCOTCH BLOODY MARY

While this might sound like the kind of drink concocted by a bartender after a cocktail too many, the combination works surprisingly well. Choose a blended Scotch with a bit of smoke to complement the tomato juice and spices, and you'll be rewarded with a very balanced flavor combination—perhaps even more so than the traditional vodka version, which adds little to no character. This is also a fun drink to order at the bar, as you are sure to get a second look from the bartender (whether from intrigue or a sense of dread). However, once the barkeep overcomes any apprehension, they will usually promise to enjoy one the next time they are on your side of the bar, so spread the gospel of this underrated cocktail far and wide.

Ingredients

a lime wedge and 2 dashes of celery salt, for the glass

2 fluid ounces blended Scotch whisky

¼ fluid ounce freshly squeezed lemon juice

1 pinch of black pepper

1 teaspoon grated horseradish

1 teaspoon soy sauce

6 dashes of Worcestershire sauce

2 dashes of hot sauce

4 fluid ounces tomato juice

a celery stalk, green olive, and lemon wedge, to garnish

Instructions

Take a pint glass and rub a lime wedge around the rim, then dip it in the celery salt. Next, add the whiskey, lemon juice, pepper, horseradish, and the sauces. Stir briefly. Add ice to the glass, top with tomato juice and stir briefly to combine. Garnish with a celery stalk, green olive, and lemon wedge.

SHIFT DRINK

Jacob Grier's other contribution to this book, the Shift Drink, was inspired by the two things bartenders often reach for at the end of their shift: whiskey and Fernet-Branca. A "shift drink" is the free drink that bartenders and other restaurant and bar staff often receive at the end of their shift as a thank you from the house for their hard work. This cocktail marries these two popular choices for shift drinks and complements them with ginger and lemon to create something that is truly memorable.

Ingredients
1 ½ fluid ounces rye whiskey
¾ fluid ounce Ginger Syrup (see page 20)
¾ fluid ounce freshly squeezed lemon juice
½ fluid ounce Fernet-Branca
a lemon twist, to garnish

Instructions
Half fill a cocktail shaker with ice. Pour in the rye whiskey, Ginger Syrup, lemon juice, and Fernet-Branca and shake until chilled. Strain over fresh ice cubes into an old-fashioned glass and garnish with a lemon twist.

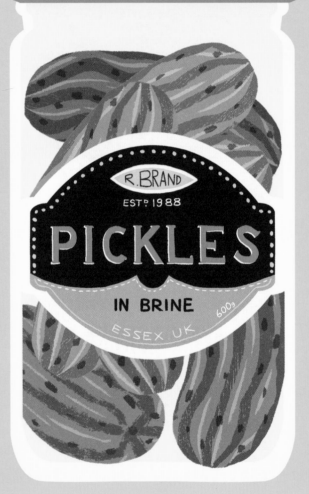

PICKLEBACK

This is one of those drinks that serves as an unofficial "bartender's handshake," as it is a very popular choice at the end of a shift. Essentially a shot of whiskey (originally it would have been Irish whiskey, but use what you enjoy) followed by a chaser of pickle brine, the Pickleback has evolved into some unusual whiskey-and-brine pairings. The combination is a classic, and cocktails don't get much easier to make than this. Even better, go into your local bar right before closing time and order one from the bartender. You'll likely get a knowing smile and a few questions about where you might bartend.

Ingredients
2 fluid ounces whiskey
2 fluid ounces pickle brine

Instructions
Pour some whiskey into a shot glass and a shot of brine into a second shot glass. Drink the whiskey, then chase it with the brine.

SWAFFORD COCKTAIL

Tom Swafford is a legend in the restaurant circles of Portland, Oregon, and the Swafford cocktail was named in his honor. Spicy rye whiskey combines with Applejack brandy to form the base spirits of the cocktail, while green chartreuse and maraschino liqueur work together to create a drink as elegantly sophisticated and timeless as the man himself. Put on some old jazz records, open a good book, and warm yourself next to a crackling fire on a cold night while you sip. Rumor has it, that's how Mr. Swafford himself enjoys this drink.

Ingredients
1 fluid ounce rye whiskey
1 fluid ounce Applejack
½ fluid ounce green chartreuse
½ fluid ounce maraschino liqueur
an orange twist, to garnish

Instructions
Pour the rye whiskey, Applejack, green chartreuse, and maraschino liqueur into a mixing glass. Add some ice and stir for 1 minute. Strain into a chilled coupe or martini glass and garnish with an orange twist.

CHARTREUSE

LIQUEUR FABRIQUÉE
PAR LES PERES   CHARTREUX

1605

Product of France

ALC 40% BY VOL   750 ML

CHARTREUSE DIFFUSION

IMPROVED WHISKEY COCKTAIL

"Professor" Jerry Thomas included this Improved Whiskey Cocktail in his original bartender's book back in 1862. You may ask yourself, "What is being improved?" Well, the answer is simple. This drink takes the classic Old-Fashioned and "improves" it with the addition of a liqueur—in this case, maraschino. The result is a cocktail that tastes great. However, unless you have a barkeep in the know, you may have to walk them through this drink. Option two, of course, is to perfect it yourself and enjoy making it at home.

Ingredients
1 sugar cube
1 dash of Angostura bitters
1 dash of Peychaud's bitters
1 dash of absinthe
1 teaspoon maraschino liqueur
2 fluid ounces bourbon
a lemon twist, to garnish

Instructions
Muddle the sugar cube with both bitters, the absinthe, and the maraschino liqueur in an old-fashioned glass. Pour in the bourbon and stir until the sugar is completely dissolved. Add some fresh ice cubes and garnish with a lemon twist.

STONE FENCE

If you only make one cocktail from this book, let this be the one. This version is from the era of the U.S. Civil War, featuring bourbon and nonalcoholic cloudy apple cider. In Colonial times this drink would have been made with rum and hard apple cider, which would have naturally fermented as it aged. The original Colonial form is a rough, "any-port-in-a-storm" kind of a drink, while this take on it is simple, elegant, and tastes like fall. Even better, you can let your guests make this for themselves during holiday cocktail parties. The proportions offered here are merely a guideline—pour a little more bourbon or get a bit heavy on the bitters, and this drink still tastes great. Even the most inexperienced hands can create this cocktail.

Ingredients
2 fluid ounces bourbon or rye whiskey
6 dashes of Angostura bitters
4 fluid ounces cloudy apple cider
a cinnamon stick and grated nutmeg, to garnish

Instructions
Pour the bourbon or whiskey into an old-fashioned glass. Add fresh ice cubes and the Angostura bitters, then top up with cloudy apple cider. Garnish with a cinnamon stick and grated nutmeg.

WHISKEY SOUR

This is a simple but delectable combination of whiskey, lemon juice, sugar, and, optionally, egg white. The egg white gives a richer mouthfeel, but either way this drink is a classic not to be missed. The Whiskey Sour is another foundational drink that allows the mixer to create some fun variations (see New York Sour on page 116). Why not try adding a barspoon of good British orange marmalade to the cocktail shaker for an interesting twist? Traditionally, this drink would be made with bourbon, but feel free to use whatever whiskey you prefer. Irish whiskey and Canadian whisky would be great choices here, and a Japanese blended whisky could work well.

Ingredients
1½ fluid ounces whiskey
¾ fluid ounce freshly squeezed lemon juice
¾ fluid ounce Simple Syrup (see page 20)
1 egg white (optional)
a lemon wheel and an amarena cherry, to garnish

Instructions
Pour the whiskey, lemon juice, Simple Syrup, and separated egg white, if using, into a cocktail shaker. Add some ice and shake vigorously for 1 minute. Strain into an old-fashioned glass filled with fresh ice cubes. Garnish with a lemon wheel and an amarena cherry.

NEW YORK SOUR

This aptly named drink is the uber-sophisticated cousin of the more down-to-earth Whiskey Sour (see page 114). Now, you may be asking yourself, "Red wine in a Whiskey Sour?" and that is a fair question. But the result is delicious, and the drink looks great when served to friends—plus, it's fairly simple to make.

Ingredients

2 fluid ounces bourbon
1 fluid ounce freshly squeezed lemon juice
1 fluid ounce Simple Syrup (see page 20)
1 egg white (optional)
½ fluid ounce red wine

Instructions

Half fill a cocktail shaker with ice. Pour in the bourbon, lemon juice, Simple Syrup, and separated egg white (optional) and shake vigorously for 1 minute. Strain into an old-fashioned glass filled with fresh ice cubes. To float the red wine, just place a barspoon over the surface of the drink and pour the wine onto the back of the spoon, allowing it to roll off and stay on top of the drink. This drink does not require a garnish but feel free to add.

BRUICHLA

PROGRESSIVE HEBRIDEAN
DISTILLERS

BRUICHLADDICH

THE
CLASSIC
LADDIE
SCOTTISH BARLEY

IT IS OUR MISSION TO
PURSUE THE ULTIMATE
PEDIGREE, PROVENANCE
AND TRACEABILITY OF
OUR RAW MATERIALS
CHIEF OF WHICH IS OUR
BARLEY AND TO PUSH
THE BOUNDARIES OF THE
CONCEPT OF TERROIR IN
ARTISANAL SINGLE
MALT WHISKY.

UNPEATED
ISLAY SINGLE MALT
SCOTCH WHISKY

DISTILLED, MATURED AND BOTTLED
UN-CHILL FILTERED AND COLOURING-FREE
AT BRUICHLADDICH DISTILLERY
ISLE OF ISLAY, SCOTLAND.
PRODUCT OF SCOTLAND.

750 ML
50% ALC/VOL.

WHISKEY FLIP

This is about as old school as cocktails get. Whiskey, egg, and sugar, shaken together into a froth that is far more than the sum of its parts. The Flip is a great drink to have in your repertoire, as it's anything but run of the mill, has a long history, and, most importantly, tastes great. In 1695, "flip" was originally used for a mixture of rum, beer, and sugar that was heated with a red-hot iron, or loggerhead. The intense heat of the iron caused the drink to froth up or "flip," hence the name. Over time, beer was replaced with whiskey, more sugar was added, an egg found its way into the mix, and the drink stopped being served hot. This recipe is for the 1800s-era version of the Flip and is easily the most suited for a modern palate.

Ingredients
2 fluid ounces whiskey
1 fluid ounce Simple Syrup (see page 20)
1 whole egg
1 nutmeg, for grating, to garnish

Instructions
Put the whiskey and Simple Syrup into a cocktail shaker, then crack in the whole egg. Add some ice and shake hard for 60 seconds. Strain into a wine glass and grate some nutmeg over the top.

IRISH FLIP

John Lermayer from Miami's Sweet Liberty created the Irish Flip in 2016. It isn't the type of drink one would expect to come from a bartender in a warm, tropical location, but this combination of Irish whiskey, chocolate bitters, Licor 43, Irish stout, and an entire egg is a very modern interpretation of the classic Flip. The key to this drink is to shake it long enough and hard enough to ensure that the ingredients are well combined.

Ingredients
1 fluid ounce Irish whiskey
1 fluid ounce Licor 43
1½ fluid ounces Irish stout
1 dash of chocolate bitters
1 whole egg
1 nutmeg, for grating, to garnish

Instructions
Half fill a cocktail shaker with ice. Pour in the Irish whiskey, Licor 43, stout, chocolate bitters, and crack in the whole egg. Shake very vigorously for 90 seconds to incorporate the egg into the drink. Strain into a martini glass and garnish with freshly grated nutmeg.

REVOLVER

The Revolver was created in the early 2000s by legendary San Francisco bartender Jon Santer, now owner of the renowned cocktail bar Prizefighter in Emeryville, California. Santer's original recipe called for a rye-heavy bourbon, but a rye whiskey also works well in this drink, adding a touch of spice that cuts through the dark coffee and orange notes. However, avoid whiskies that are too light-bodied, as the other ingredients will overwhelm the flavor.

Ingredients
2 fluid ounces rye-based bourbon
½ fluid ounce coffee liqueur
2 dashes of orange bitters
a large orange twist, to garnish

Instructions
Pour the bourbon, coffee liqueur, and orange bitters into a mixing glass. Add some ice and stir for 1 minute. Strain into a chilled coupe or martini glass and garnish with a large orange twist.

TONKA COCKTAIL

Created in 2010 at Schumann's Bar in Munich, Germany by Klaus St. Rainer, the Tonka Cocktail is an inventive Japanese whisky-based drink. Pairing the blended Japanese whisky with sweet vermouth and chocolate vodka creates a rich, complex drink that shows just how mixable Japanese whisky can be. Notes of chocolate and orange are dominant flavors in this drink, but it is interesting to taste the secondary flavors of vanilla and caramel from the whisky and marvel at so many layers in one drink.

Ingredients
2 fluid ounces Japanese blended whisky
1 fluid ounce sweet vermouth
½ fluid ounce chocolate vodka
2 dashes of Angostura bitters
a flamed orange peel (see page 60), to garnish

Instructions
Combine the Japanese blended whisky, sweet vermouth, chocolate vodka, and Angostura bitters in a mixing glass. Add some ice and stir for 60 seconds. Strain into a chilled martini glass and garnish with a flamed orange peel.

SMOKY ROBINSON

Not to be confused with the legendary R&B and soul singer Smokey Robinson, this drink combines whiskey with the smoke of mezcal, tequila's bad-boy cousin. Add in some Maple-Spiced Simple Syrup and there is a lot going on in this drink. This is one to sit and savor on a crisp fall night, perhaps with a little Smokey Robinson playing in the background.

Ingredients

1½ fluid ounces Tennessee whiskey (such as George Dickel)
½ fluid ounce mezcal
¾ fluid ounce Maple-Spiced Simple Syrup (see page 20)
¾ fluid ounce freshly squeezed lemon juice
a lemon twist, to garnish

Instructions

First make the Maple-Spiced Simple Syrup (see page 20).

In a cocktail shaker, combine the Tennessee whiskey, mezcal, Maple-Spiced Simple Syrup, and lemon juice. Add some ice and shake. Strain into an ice-filled rocks glass and garnish with a lemon twist.

MILK PUNCH

(Serves 2)

This is a classic drink from New Orleans, where there is no wrong time to order one but the majority are consumed over brunch. And it really is a perfect brunch cocktail; the addition of some milk and sweetener makes it a great pairing with traditional beignets, waffles, or a nice stack of pancakes. Start your weekend right, like a true New Orleanian—with a Milk Punch in one hand and a cup of chicory coffee in the other.

Ingredients
2 fluid ounces bourbon
½ fluid ounce Simple Syrup (see page 20)
4 fluid ounces whole milk
1–2 drops of vanilla extract
1 nutmeg, for grating, to garnish

Instructions
Add the bourbon, Simple Syrup, milk, and vanilla extract to a cocktail shaker. Add some ice and shake for 1 minute. Strain into 2 chilled coupe or martini glasses and garnish with grated nutmeg.

Milk

FRESH

PURE
VANILLA
EXTRACT

CLARIFIED MILK PUNCH

(Serves 40 x 3-fluid-ounce servings)

While the Milk Punch hearkens back to yesteryear, the Clarified Milk Punch is a modern interpretation that is definitely worth the work. Probably the most complex preparation in this book, this recipe is also the most rewarding, as it offers a peek behind the curtain at one of the techniques that many avant-garde bartenders use with molecular mixology—milk washing. While it may sound absurd, this technique works well, creating a drink that is both visually stunning and delicious. There is no way you can fail to impress your guests with this cocktail.

Ingredients
11 lemons
24 fluid ounces bourbon
24 fluid ounces blended Scotch whisky
16 fluid ounces freshly squeezed lemon juice
32 fluid ounces water
1¾ cups superfine sugar
1 whole nutmeg
2 cinnamon sticks
1 star anise
24 fluid ounces whole milk

Instructions
Day one: Peel the lemons with a Y-shaped vegetable peeler, avoiding the bitter white pith. Combine the peels with the whiskies in a jar or bowl, cover, and let it rest in the refrigerator for 24 hours.

Day two: Strain the peels out of the whiskey mixture, add the lemon juice, sugar, and water, and stir until the sugar is dissolved. Grate the nutmeg and break up the cinnamon sticks and star anise into the mix. Bring the milk to a boil in a large pan, and as soon as it is boiling, add the spirits and lemon juice mixture. Stir a bit to dissolve any remaining sugar, then turn off the heat and let the milk curdle. Let it sit with a cover on the pan for a couple of hours. Using lots of cheesecloth, strain the milk solids out of the punch. Working in small batches, run the punch through the cheesecloth, regularly rinsing the cloth as needed. Cover and refrigerate the punch until any remaining sediment settles (about 2 hours). Ladle the punch into a clean bottle or serving container and keep refrigerated. To serve, pour over a large ice cube or drink neat in an old-fashioned glass.

EGGNOG

(Serves 8 x 4-fluid-ounce servings)

Originally a British tradition, this drink eventually found its way to the United States. Usually consumed around Christmas, Eggnog is descended from "posset"—a hot drink made with ale. The origin of the name "Eggnog" remains elusive; some think "nog" was a style of beer brewed in England, while others believe it is descended from "noggin"—a small wooden mug used for consuming ale in the 1800s. Whatever the lineage, Eggnog is a holiday staple and one worth mastering. This recipe will yield an Eggnog far superior to any commercial varieties and is sure to impress your friends and neighbors. This drink is best made a few days before serving, so that the flavors have a chance to get to know each other. The extra time and effort are worth it.

Ingredients

4 large eggs
generous ¾ cup granulated sugar
1 teaspoon grated nutmeg
⅛ teaspoon ground allspice
⅛ teaspoon ground cloves
½ teaspoon ground cinnamon
2 fluid ounces Hennessy VSOP cognac
2 fluid ounces Grand Marnier
4 fluid ounces Bulleit bourbon
12 fluid ounces whole milk
8 fluid ounces heavy cream

Instructions

Crack the eggs into a large blender and pulse until blended. Then slowly work your way down the ingredients list (in order), adding each item until they are all incorporated, for a total blending time of about 5 minutes. Serve immediately in punch cups or glass mugs with grated nutmeg to add as garnish.

OPEN HERE---▶

FESTIVE & DELICIOUS

EGG NOG

WITH BOURBON,

HENNESSY & GRAND MARNIER

ISLAY HOT CHOCOLATE

This drink is an easy gem that is perfect for a very cold night. Choose any Islay Scotch whisky that you like (note for any non-Scots: Islay is pronounced "Eye-luh" not "iss-lay"!) and combine with good-quality hot chocolate. It's simple, easy, and delicious, and the sweetness of the chocolate tempers the bold smoke and peat that Islay Scotch is famous for. Rumor has it that this is Santa's favorite tipple after a hard night of delivering presents, so don't be afraid to substitute this for his usual glass of milk.

Ingredients
2 fluid ounces Islay single malt Scotch whisky
4 fluid ounces good-quality brewed hot chocolate
whipped cream, to garnish

Instructions
Pour the Islay Scotch into a coffee mug and top with the hot chocolate prepared according to packet instructions or personal preference. Garnish with whipped cream just before serving.

IRISH COFFEE

This cocktail can trace its origin back to Shannon Airport in the 1950s, where it was first created by Joe Sheridan to warm up a group of cold and travel-weary Americans. Back home, two San Franciscans, writer Stanton Delaplane and Jack Koeppler—the owner of a local bar, called the Buena Vista—set out to recreate the drink they had first tasted back in Shannon. Eventually, the two men hit on the perfect combination of coffee, sugar, Irish whiskey (no substitutions, please!), and whipped cream. The drink became such a hit at the Buena Vista (which serves up to two thousand Irish coffees a day) that this increase in demand eventually helped to revive the flagging fortunes of the Irish whiskey industry. All from one little drink. So while you sip, take a moment to reflect on how two friends half a world away may have inadvertently saved the Irish whiskey industry and raise a toast to Misters Delaplane and Koeppler.

Ingredients

1 ½ fluid ounces Irish whiskey
½ fluid ounce Brown Sugar Simple Syrup (see page 20)
4 fluid ounces freshly brewed black coffee
whipped cream, to garnish

Instructions

Into a heatproof mug, pour the Irish whiskey and Simple Syrup. Top with the freshly brewed coffee. Then, using a barspoon, carefully pour whipped cream off the back of the spoon onto the surface of the coffee so that the cream floats. Serve hot.

IRISH

COFFEE

IRISH WHISKEY
DUBLIN
ROE & CO

BLENDED IRISH WHISKEY

PRODUCT
OF
IRELAND

BATCH
3

BOTTLE NO.
1236

70cl   45%abv

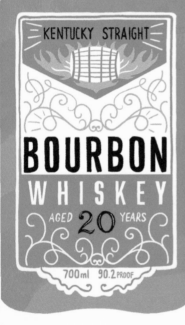

HOT TODDY

This is a drink that has been used to take the chill off one's bones and to cure what ails since perhaps the very creation of whiskey itself. It is the kind of drink that would have been served in 18th-century taverns and inns across Scotland, with the mugful of water heated by a large piece of iron called a loggerhead, which was kept in the fireplace just for the purpose. But don't let its simplicity fool you—this drink is far more than the basic ingredients. Once you've mastered the toddy, feel free to play around with variations. You can easily substitute the hot water for your favorite tea (I recommend Earl Grey) or switch the honey for another sweetener.

Ingredients
1 fluid ounce honey
½ fluid ounce freshly squeezed lemon juice
1 ½ fluid ounces whiskey
2 fluid ounces hot water
a cinnamon stick, to garnish
½ lemon wheel studded with cloves, to garnish

Instructions
Into a heatproof glass mug, pour the honey, lemon juice, and whiskey. Add the hot water and stir to combine. Garnish with a cinnamon stick and the half lemon wheel studded with cloves. Serve hot.

LONDON FOG

(Serves 24 x 4-fluid-ounce servings)

This classic yet simple ice cream–based drink is perfect for parties. All you need is a punch bowl, some vanilla ice cream, and coffee (cold-brew works best, but don't let it prevent you from making this if you don't have any around), decent whiskey and a ladle. Questions about the origin of this drink abound, but many credit computer programmer Ward Cunningham, developer of the world's first wiki, for popularizing the drink by serving it as his signature cocktail at holiday gatherings. No matter how it came about, this is a great party drink that is certain to impress a crowd.

Ingredients
½ gallon drippy vanilla ice cream (leave out of the freezer for at least 35 minutes)
16 fluid ounces bourbon
16 fluid ounces cold-brewed coffee

Instructions
Combine the ice cream, bourbon, and coffee in a punch bowl. Stir occasionally as the ice cream melts. Serve in punch cups. This cocktail is to be drunk, but a spoon can also be used.

INDEX

CREDITS

Lance J. Mayhew would like to thank:
For Amelia, Samuel, and Charlotte, my pride and joy. Chase your
dreams. Raena, my rock, I love you like a tomato. Mom, Dad, Wayne,
and Denise, thank you for all that you have done and continue to do.
Richard DellaPenna, Joseph "Moose" Morante, Dave Cupps, and Chris
Curtis—the bartenders who inspired and mentored me. Jacob Grier
and Ky Belk, great bartenders and even better people. Father Mike
Biewend and the entire Madeleine Parish and School for their unceasing
support and love. John Zimmer and Jennifer Moore, Paul and Manda
Hardy, Steve Mendiola, and Jason and Grace Thornton. If the measure
of a person is the friends one has, then I am a very lucky man. Takesuke
Naito and Mike Dunne, thanks for putting up with me. Terry Boyd and
Matt Wilcox, who make radio seem far easier than it really is and gave
me the chance to make cocktails on air and tell embarrassing stories
about myself. Caitlin Doyle, the best editor I've ever had the pleasure
to work with; thank you for your patience and kindness. And lastly,
thank you dear reader, without whom this book would just be words on
paper. *"You miss 100% of the shots you don't take."— Wayne Gretzky*

Ruby Taylor would like to thank:
For all the love, support (and drinks) always; Katie Price,
Nancy Edmondson, Billie Alder, Ella Antebi, Roxanne
Simmonds, Pema Seely, Ellie Yates, Anita Kershaw.